Old Fashioned Magick:
Cocktails Under Quarantine

Bryson Granger

AuthorHouse™
1663 Liberty Drive
Bloomington, IN 47403
www.authorhouse.com
Phone: 833-262-8899

Because of the dynamic nature of the Internet, any web addresses or links contained in this book may have changed
since publication and may no longer be valid. The views expressed in this work are solely those of the author and do
not necessarily reflect the views of the publisher, and the publisher hereby disclaims any responsibility for them.

Any people depicted in stock imagery provided by Getty Images are models,
and such images are being used for illustrative purposes only.
Certain stock imagery © Getty Images.

This book is printed on acid-free paper.

ISBN: 978-1-6655-1119-3 (sc)
      978-1-6655-1120-9 (e)

Library of Congress Control Number: 2020925190

Print information available on the last page.

Published by AuthorHouse 02/23/2021

To whosoever finds this book, may your actions bring about the positive change you seek, and may the rest of your days be spent in prosperity and your years in contentment.

Table of Contents

The view from my window has changed since March. Traffic that once flooded the streets of San Diego has almost become lost in time, along with human interaction. Seclusion has started to set in, and ignoring it hasn't helped. The noticeable wrinkle seemingly left on my mind only becomes easier to manage with a tumbler in hand.

These past few months amid the 2020 pandemic have been like a page straight out of a science fiction novel. COVID-19 is still running amok, and quarantine is still very much a part of our lives. Things were looking better a month or so ago, but there is now talk of a second wave of coronavirus and possibly even a second stay-at-home order.

Here in Southern California, we are right in the thick of it. Face masks are required for entry into any store or public place, and just as recently as yesterday, laws have been enacted to require face masks outside of your home in general. The floors at the grocery stores have arrow decals pointing out which direction to walk and telling customers where to stand during checkout. Social distancing of six feet or more keeps both friends and strangers apart, and there doesn't quite seem to be an end in sight. It's a very strange time here on planet Earth.

I thought, *Hey, with all the extra time at home, it's the perfect excuse to become more acquainted with my home bar.* The liquor cabinet in my living room has been fully stocked for quite some time, but as 2020 goes on and with a global pandemic forcing most to keep to themselves, the time has come. I've had my bitters, liquors, vermouths, and liqueurs staring back at me over the past month, and I say there's no time like the present.

Originally, I wanted to do a list of cocktails that you could pull together easily without too much work—a quarantine guide. And ultimately, that's what this is. This book does have many classic cocktails, some with my own spin, along with a few of my own signature concoctions. There are some simple syrup recipes in the back of the book that can be made ahead of time as well, so I'd recommend taking a look there and maybe even doing some easy preparations to make your drinking experience that much better. There are a few cocktails in here that might have an ingredient or two you'll have to track down, but most of these drinks you'll be able to pull together without too much effort.

Let's put those bottles that you haven't touched in a while to good use! Of course, a global stay-at-home order from our government makes it that much easier to put this rule book into action, but whether for quarantine survival or a Saturday night with your friends, it'll be your best friend behind the bar.

While certain bartenders are starting to see a light on the horizon with a return date, going back to work full-force with masks and rubber gloves, most (myself included) are sitting at home twiddling our thumbs until things mellow out again. This is essentially a guide on how to survive quarantine with your home bar to keep you company. Let's pour ourselves a stiffy and jump right in.

Old Fashioned

1/4 ounce Demerara syrup (7 ml)

2 ounces rye (60 ml)

4 dashes Angostura bitters

2 dashes Bitter Truth orange bitters

1 large ice cube

orange peel, for garnish

2 maraschino cherries, for garnish

I. In a rocks glass, combine syrup, rye, and bitters.
II. Add a large ice cube and stir for 20 seconds.
III. Flamed orange zest over cocktail. (Light a match, twist orange peel to "express" citrus into flame over cocktail [outer peel facing drink].)
IV. Garnish with orange peel and cherries on a bamboo pick.

To me, it says something about who you are as a drinker if you know how you prefer your old fashioned. This classic cocktail has varied slightly over the years, but many bars out there stay true to a good classic recipe. The old fashioned cocktail came about around the year 1806, and although its popularity has come in waves and it somehow found its way through Prohibition, it has become the most commonly ordered drink on the planet. You'll usually find it made with bourbon, but we'll make ours with rye whiskey.

Did You Know?

In the early 1800s, a cocktail was simply a spirit mixed with sweetener, bitters, and water, no ice. By the late 1870s, people started referring to this cocktail as an "old fashioned" because it was a cocktail made the old-fashioned way!

Whiskey Sour

1/2 ounce simple syrup (15 ml)

3/4 ounce fresh lemon juice (22 ml)

2 ounces rye (60 ml)

egg white

3 rocks

3 dashes Angostura bitters

I. In a shaker, combine simple syrup, lemon juice, rye, and egg white. Dry shake. (Shake without ice.)
II. *Now* add ice, shake vigorously and strain into a rocks glass over rocks.
III. Garnish with bitters.

The whiskey sour is always a great choice and one of the most recognizable cocktails on earth. Bar patrons always get stoked when you place their sour down in front of them all nice and frothy. Don't be afraid of the egg white; it's more just for texture. They say that this delicious beverage dates back to the 1700s, but it wasn't until years later that it was put in Jerry Thomas' *The Bartenders Guide* from 1862. It's the perfect all-around cocktail—just please leave out the sweet and sour.

Did You Know?

Whiskey sour is one of those cocktails that has had a million different versions that have popped up since its inception. If you substitute maple syrup for simple syrup, you will have a filibuster. If you substitute honey for simple syrup, you have a gold rush. Red wine on top of the original recipe (minus the egg white) gives us a New York sour.

New York Sour

1/2 ounce simple syrup (15 ml)

1 ounce fresh lemon juice (30 ml)

2 ounces scotch (60 ml)

splash malbec (or another favorite fruity red wine)

I. In a shaker, combine simple syrup, lemon juice, and scotch.
II. Shake and strain into a rocks glass over ice.
III. Top with malbec. No garnish.

Speaking of the New York sour! A whiskey sour with a red wine float and no egg white. If you wanna get fancy, you can gently pour malbec over the back side of the spoon to keep it as its own clean layer on top of the cocktail. The New York sour came around in the year of 1880 out of Chicago and has had many names since its first appearance. Whatever it is you call this bad boy, you can't deny its rightful place as an ideal cocktail under quarantine.

Did You Know?

Whisky is actually spelled without an *e* in most parts of the world. This includes Canadian, Scotch, and Japanese whiskies as well, whereas the United States and Ireland spell theirs with an *e—whiskey*. Weird, right? Alcohol and whiskey laws can be quite interesting from country to country. From new or used barrels, to the type of wood used to make them, to how long the alcohol has been aged, there are laws behind everything from the *bourbon* label down to the spelling of *whiskey*.

Vieux Carré

1/4 ounce Bénédictine D.O.M. (7 ml)

1 ounce sweet vermouth (30 ml)

1 ounce Cognac (30 ml)

1 ounce rye (30 ml)

2 dashes Angostura bitters

2 dashes Peychaud's bitters

frozen cherry, for garnish

I. In a mixing glass, combine Bénédictine, vermouth, Cognac, rye, and bitters.
II. Add ice, stir for 20 seconds and strain into a chilled coupe (or martini glass).
III. Garnish with cherry on a bamboo pick.

This New Orleans classic comes with Bénédictine D.O.M., sweet vermouth, Cognac rye whiskey, and bitters. What a combination. Bénédictine may be an ingredient that you'll have to make a liquor store run for, but this classy cocktail will totally be worth it. Originally created at the Swan Bar located at the Hotel Monteleone, which later changed its name to the Carousel Bar. (A circular bar which spun very slowly while you sat at it.) The bar has become world famous for not only their spinning bar top, but also the many classic cocktails that have gotten their start there. This one was first mixed in the 1930s, and it was around the same time that it was printed in *Famous New Orleans Drinks and How to Mix 'Em*, by Stanley Arthur. I can't recommend the Vieux Carré enough.

Did You Know?

The Vieux Carré's name comes from the French phrase meaning "old square," which referred to the French Quarter, the oldest neighborhood in New Orleans.

WhiskeySmash

5 mint leaves

3 lemon wedges

1 ounce simple syrup (30 ml)

2 ounces bourbon (60 ml)

lemon peel, for garnish

mint sprig, for garnish

I. In a shaker, muddle mint leaves, lemon wedges, and simple syrup. (Use a muddler or the end of a wooden spoon to press the herbs and citrus to extract their oils.)
II. Add bourbon and ice, give it a quick shake, and dump contents into a rocks glass.
III. Express lemon zest over cocktail. (Twist lemon peel to "express" citrus over cocktail [outer peel facing drink].)
IV. Garnish with lemon peel and mint sprig.

The whiskey smash is like the mint julep but without the extra step of crushing ice and with the addition of citrus. The original whiskey smash appeared in Jerry Thomas' *The Bartenders Guide* in 1862. The drink has made an appearance in plenty of movies at this point, which has been a big reason why it has gained so much popularity over the years. With just a few easy ingredients, this cocktail is already quarantine-ready.

Did You Know?

In the late 1800s, one Harry Johnson, who is credited as the first to start writing down his recipes, published the original recipe for the whiskey smash, but under a different name. Harry Johnson's whiskey smash was just a cool concoction of sugar, water, mint, ice, and a wine glass of whiskey. He added that to a glass with seasonal fruits and served it with a julep strainer. This would eventually evolve into the cocktail that we know and love. Thanks Harry Johnson.

Hot Toddy

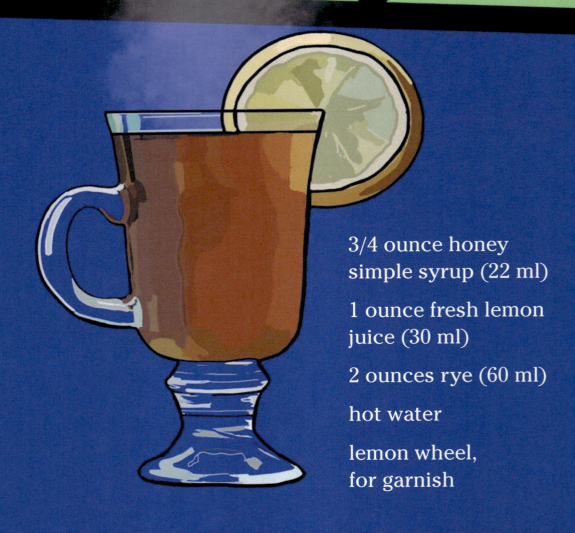

3/4 ounce honey
simple syrup (22 ml)

1 ounce fresh lemon
juice (30 ml)

2 ounces rye (60 ml)

hot water

lemon wheel,
for garnish

I. In a tulip, combine simple syrup, lemon juice, and rye.
II. Fill with hot water.
III. Garnish with lemon wheel.

Feeling under the weather? A nice hot toddy will make you forget all about it. Hey, even if you have suspicions, you might whip yourself up one of these bad boys as a preventative measure. Better safe than sorry! Apparently, they've been making hot toddys in India since the 1600s, although under a different name. There are actually multiple stories of where this one got its start. But with only a few ingredients, of course it has been a commonly made drink by people all over the world for hundreds of years— and now it's a quarantine favorite.

Did You Know?

There are certain Scots that swear that the only way to make a true hot toddy is by drawing water from Tod's Well in Edinburgh! Now there's a mission for ya once quarantine's over.

Rob Roy

1/2 ounce sweet vermouth (15 ml)

2 ounces scotch (60 ml)

3 dashes Angostura bitters

1 maraschino cherry, for garnish

I. In a mixing glass, combine vermouth, scotch, and bitters.
II. Add ice, stir for 20 seconds and strain into a chilled coupe (or martini glass).
III. Garnish with cherry on a bamboo pick.

The Rob Roy cocktail will always hold a special place in my heart. After starting to bartend, I was all about them. It was hilarious. I looked like a sixty-year-old man each time I ordered one, but it's quick and easy to pull together and tastes amazing, which is why it's on our list. A Manhattan with scotch, it was created in 1894 at the Waldorf Astoria hotel in Manhattan, New York. The Rob Roy cocktail was apparently unveiled at an operetta that was based on a Scottish folk hero of the same name.

Did You Know?

Just like with a Manhattan, you can make your Rob Roy a *perfect* Rob Roy by using 1/4 ounce sweet vermouth and 1/4 ounce dry vermouth.

Penicillin

3/4 ounce simple syrup mixture (22 ml) (half honey simple syrup, half ginger simple syrup)

1 ounce fresh lemon juice (30 ml)

2 ounces blended scotch (60 ml)

1 giant ice cube

1/4 ounce peaty single malt scotch (7 ml)

candied ginger, for garnish

lemon twist, for garnish

I. Add a giant ice cube to rocks glass.
II. In a shaker, combine simple syrup mixture, lemon juice, and blended scotch.
III. Shake and strain into a rocks glass over ice.
IV. Spray single malt scotch over cocktail (or top off with 1/4 ounce).
V. Garnish with candied ginger and/or lemon twist.

Another favorite right up there with the old fashioned. A little atomizer spray bottle is a great way to put your favorite peaty single malt on top to get those aromatics rolling, but pouring a quarter ounce on top works great too. This amazing beverage was originally created by an Australian bartender named Sam Ross at New York bar, Milk and Honey in the early 2000s. The penicillin cocktail blends fresh lemon juice, fresh ginger, and honey perfectly, topped off with a single malt scotch. Delicious.

Did You Know?

If you don't want to make a ginger simple syrup ahead of time, you can make honey simple (recipe in the back). Use a full 3/4 ounce honey simple and muddle a piece of ginger in place of ginger simple syrup. (Use a muddler or the end of a wooden spoon to press ginger to extract the oils.) Shake and double-strain!

Brooklyn

3/4 ounce dry vermouth (22 ml)

1/4 ounce Amer Picon (or Torani Amer, Golden Moon Amer dit Picon) (7 ml)

1/4 ounce maraschino liqueur (7 ml)

2 ounces rye (60 ml)

I. In a mixing glass, combine vermouth, Amer Picon, maraschino liqueur, and rye.
II. Add ice, stir for 20 seconds and strain into a chilled coupe (or martini glass). No garnish.

Here's another great rye drink coming straight from the boroughs of New York City, along with a host of other cocktails. It's basically a Manhattan, but with Canadian whisky, dry vermouth, maraschino liqueur (I use Luxardo), and Amer Picon (a French aperitif), which are what makes this cocktail so unique. This cocktail disappeared for a while due to Prohibition, but has made quite the comeback in the last thirty years. The Brooklyn cocktail is always a solid choice.

Did You Know?

Amer Picon is a French aperitif and is actually a total pain to find in the United States, or at least in California. If you can get your hands on one, great; if not, we just need to grab a different aperitif. Torani Amer works great, as well as Golden Moon Amer dit Picon, which is said to be about the same recipe as Amer Picon but with a higher alcohol content. Golden Moon Amer dit Picon is more expensive, but both should be relatively easy to find.

Boulevardier

1 ounce sweet vermouth (or Amer Picon) (30 ml)

1 ounce Campari (30 ml)

1 ounce rye (30 ml)

orange peel, for garnish

I. In a mixing glass, combine vermouth, Campari, and rye.
II. Add ice, stir for 20 seconds and strain into a chilled coupe (or stir in rocks glass).
III. Express flamed orange zest over cocktail. (Light a match, twist orange peel to "express" citrus into flame over cocktail [outer peel facing drink].)
IV. Garnish with flamed orange peel.

Oh how beautiful: a negroni with rye whiskey substituted for gin. This one also has a flamed orange peel, which helps liven up the cocktail a little bit and gives you some more aromatic love. Straight from Paris, it was created by an American born writer named Erskine Gwynne, who had packed up his things to head for France by the 1920s. He founded a monthly magazine in Paris under the name *The Boulevardier*. The drink was soon to follow under the publication with the same name.

Did You Know?

One of the earliest forms of this recipe popped up in *Barflies and Cocktails* by Harry MacElhone, another American who made the move to Europe. MacElhone was a former head bartender at the Plaza Hotel. *Barflies and Cocktails* included over three hundred classic cocktail recipes which were written as a means of safekeeping throughout Prohibition.

MintJulep

5 sprigs mint (use 1 as garnish)

1 ounce simple syrup (30 ml)

crushed ice

2 1/2 ounces bourbon (75 ml)

mint sprig, for garnish

I.   In a rocks glass, muddle 4 sprigs of mint and simple syrup. (Use a muddler or the end of a wooden spoon to press the herbs to extract their oils.)
II. Fill with crushed ice.
III. Add bourbon and pile more crushed ice on top to create an ice dome.
IV. Garnish with mint sprig.

The mint julep is a cousin of the whiskey smash, although the julep has been around for much longer. It was originally used as a cure for an upset stomach. A cocktail straight from the Kentucky Derby in the 1700s, the mint julep comes with crushed ice; you can either put a brick of ice under a towel or cheesecloth to crush it with a bar mallet or use your bar spoon to smack against the ice cubes to crack them up into smaller pieces. Drink your mint julep as the crushed ice melts.

Did You Know?

Originally, this cocktail was made with Cognac, but over time it has been known to come with bourbon— and up to 3 ounces of it!

Godfather

1 ounce amaretto (30 ml)

2 ounces blended scotch (60 ml)

I.   In a rocks glass, combine amaretto and scotch.
II. Add ice and stir for 20 seconds. No garnish.

This one is a real easy one, with just scotch and amaretto, which definitely puts it on the quarantine map. Just two ingredients! Two! The godfather was said to have gained popularity around the 1970s, however, bartender Donato Antone, who also claims to have invented everything from the White Russian to the kamikaze, claims he created the godfather as early as the 1950s! The godfather is a damn fine choice, and already quarantine-ready!

Did You Know?

The Disaronno brand claims that amaretto was the favorite drink of Marlon Brando, who played the actual godfather, Don Vito Corleone in the movie *The Godfather,* released in 1972.

Rusty Nail

3/4 ounce Drambuie (22 ml)

1 1/2 ounces scotch (44 ml)

3 rocks

lemon peel, for garnish

I. In a rocks glass, combine Drambuie and scotch.
II. Add rocks and stir for 20 seconds.
III. Express lemon zest over cocktail. (Twist lemon peel to "express" citrus over cocktail [outer peel facing drink].)
IV. Garnish with lemon peel.

Can't go wrong with a rusty nail—that is if you're a scotch lover. This one comes with scotch and Drambuie, which is a heather honey scotch. This is a heavy-hitter and another truly amazing drink. If you can hunt down your bottle of Drambuie, this one is high on the quarantine charts. The rusty nail is another that has been around for quite some time, although this cocktail didn't really pick up until the 1970s. It's a super simple cocktail, but a classic all the way.

Did You Know?

If you're a beer person, you can make a rusty *ale* by just adding a shot of Drambuie to your favorite beer!

The Bear of Bad News

3/4 ounce honey simple syrup (22 ml)

3/4 ounce fresh lemon juice (22 ml)

2 ounces scotch (60 ml)

2 dashes R&D cherry apple bitters

dehydrated lemon wheel, for garnish

cinnamon stick, for garnish

I. In a shaker, combine simple syrup, lemon juice, scotch, and bitters.
II. Shake and strain into a rocks glass over ice.
III. Garnish with dehydrated lemon wheel and burnt cinnamon stick (light the end on fire and let the cocktail smoke as you sip).

Feed this one to your favorite party pooper; every friend group has one. It's hard to be in a bad mood with one of these bad boys in hand. This festive cocktail does have a tinge of cinnamon, for obvious reasons, but it's a safe bet all year round. Turn that frown upside down with the bear of bad news.

Did you know?

You could also take the bear of bad news one step further and pre-soak the cinnamon in 151 rum! Right before you start sipping, grab your cinnamon stick with tongs and light it on fire, then drop it into the drink to kill the flame. This will also add some smokiness to the cocktail!

Cold Coffee With a Python

1/2 ounce honey simple syrup (15 ml)

1 ounce cold brew (30 ml)

2 ounces bourbon (60 ml)

2 dashes Angostura bitters

3 dashes R&D sarsaparilla bitters

ground nutmeg, for garnish

I. In a shaker, combine simple syrup, cold brew, bourbon, and bitters.
II. Shake and strain into a chilled coupe (or martini glass).
III. Sprinkle ground nutmeg over the cocktail for garnish.

Originally, this cocktail got its start at the toss of the mixology dice. Literally. Ingredients engraved into dice that you toss while crossing your fingers and hoping for the best. I was prepared to make some adjustments if need be, but this one turned out perfect just the way it was. If you're getting an early start, this one will help keep your morning nice and smooth.

Did you know?

Nutmeg actually has a number of health benefits! From its antioxidants to anti-inflammatory properties, to antibacterial properties! Nutmeg is said to boost libido, fight off cancer, boost brain health, and the list goes on!

The Poisoned Monkey

1/4 ounce amaretto (7 ml)

2 ounces rye (60 ml)

2 dashes Fee Brothers black walnut bitters

1 dash R&D sarsaparilla bitters

orange peel, for garnish

I.   In a rocks glass, combine amaretto, rye, and bitters.
II. Add ice and stir for 20 seconds.
III. Express orange zest over cocktail. (Twist orange peel to "express" citrus over cocktail [outer peel facing drink].)
IV. Garnish with orange peel.

A drink I first made a couple years back, which started off as more of a spin on the old fashioned, and as time went on, amaretto and some other ingredients found their way into the drink. The amaretto and sarsaparilla bitters with a little orange on the nose are what make this one so addicting. A true personal favorite to this day. Everyday. Get bitten by the poisoned monkey and you'll never look back.

Did you know?

Black walnut bitters may sound off-putting, however, it goes very well with this cocktail and will probably surprise you! It's actually a terrific addition to a wide variety of cocktails and helps to mellow out the drink quite a bit with notes of cola and cocoa, and a sour cherry aroma!

Margarita

kosher salt

1/2 ounce agave syrup (15 ml)

1 ounce fresh lime juice (30 ml)

1/2 ounce Cointreau (or triple sec) (15 ml)

2 ounces silver tequila (or reposado) (60 ml)

lime wedge, for garnish

I.   Salt rim of a rocks glass (or margarita glass) first. Or don't.
II. In a shaker, combine agave syrup, lime juice, Cointreau, and tequila.
III. Shake and strain into glass over ice.
IV. Garnish with lime wedge.

For years, my mom used to buy the Jose Cuervo premix jug where you dump it on ice and call it a day. That is, until years later, when I got Mom her own shaker tin and set of bar supplies. She never looked back. The margarita dates back to the 1930s, but it was in 1937 that it appeared in a bar book under the name of the 'picador' cocktail. Fast forward a hundred years, and the margarita is one of the most commonly ordered drinks in the world.

Did You Know?

You can add a half ounce of Grand Marnier on top after making your cocktail to make it a Cadillac Margarita! Grandma is your friend.

Skinny Margarita

kosher salt

2 ounces silver tequila (60 ml)

2 1/2 ounces skinny mix (75 ml) (1 1/2 ounces fresh lime juice and 1 ounce agave syrup)

lime wedge, for garnish

I. Salt rim of rocks glass (or margarita glass).
II. Add tequila and fill to the rim with ice.
III. Top off with skinny mix. (Build cocktail in a shaker and shake first if skinny mix is not premade, strain over ice.)
IV. Garnish with lime wedge.

Since the creation of the classic margarita, there have been countless spin-offs, and over the years, the term *skinny* was used when there was little or no triple sec and only a few ingredients. The skinny margarita is actually my personal favorite margarita. I like to make my skinny mix in advance so I don't have to worry about measuring agave and lime for each drink. The skinny mix ratio should be around 1 1/2 parts lime juice to 1 part agave syrup. (Quick agave syrup recipe in back.)

Did You Know?

The term *margarita* is Spanish for "daisy!"

Paloma

pinch of sea salt

1/2 ounce simple syrup (15 ml)

1/2 ounce fresh lime juice (15 ml)

1 ounce fresh grapefruit
juice (30 ml)

2 ounces tequila (60 ml)

soda water

lime wedge, for garnish

I.   In a shaker, combine salt, simple syrup, lime juice, grapefruit juice, and tequila.
II. Shake and strain into a collins glass over ice.
III. Top with soda water.
IV. Garnish with lime wedge.

This beautiful tequila cocktail is said to have gotten its start in the 1800s right along with so many other greats. Some like their palomas made with Squirt. I personally like mine with soda water, grapefruit juice, and simple syrup—and I hate grapefruit juice. The history of the paloma is complete speculation at this point, although some refer to the legendary Don Javier Delgado Corona, owner and bartender of La Capilla, in Tequila, Mexico, as the first to put this one together. It's the perfect day drink.

Did You Know?

Some believe that this cocktail was named after *La Paloma* or "The Dove," a popular folk song composed in the early 1860s.

The Green Nile

1 sprig cilantro

1/2 ounce jalapeño simple syrup (15 ml)

1/4 ounce agave syrup (7 ml)

1 ounce fresh lime juice (30 ml)

2 ounces silver tequila (60 ml)

2 dashes R&D fire bitters

I.   In a shaker, combine cilantro, simple syrup, agave syrup, lime juice, tequila, and bitters.
II. Shake and double-strain into a chilled coupe (or martini glass). No garnish.

Here's a great cocktail to put that jalapeño simple syrup and fire bitters to the test. Just enough spice for you to get your fix, but it's a smooth sipper. No muddling is necessary, and let's make it a small cilantro sprig, so not to overpower the drink. No garnish on this baby.

Did you know?

Cilantro is said to be a useful ingredient in many different ways! Having cilantro in your diet, in one form or another, can clear up your skin, lead to weight loss, boosty energy, help strengthen hair, prevent heart disease, and more!

MezcalMule

1 1/2 ounces ginger puree (44 ml)

1/2 ounce fresh lime juice (15 ml)

2 ounces mezcal (60 ml)

2 dashes Angostura bitters

ginger beer

lime wheel,
for garnish

I. In a shaker, combine ginger puree, lime juice, mezcal, and bitters.
II. Shake and strain into a copper mug over ice.
III. Top with ginger beer.
IV. Garnish with lime wheel.

I suppose it depends on what mood I'm in, but usually, if there's a mezcal cocktail option on the menu, it catches my eye right off the bat. The process of creating mezcal requires agave to be roasted with wood and charcoal, whereas with tequila, it's steamed before it is distilled. This is what gives mezcal its smoky taste, which pairs excellently with the ginger puree and lime juice in this mule variation. There are quite a few ways to throw this one together. Here's how I like it.

Did You Know?

Production of tequila and mezcal is strictly limited to Mexico, but agave plants themselves are most commonly grown from the southwestern part of the U.S. through the northern part of South America. And they all have different life cycles—ranging from five to thirty years based on their location!

Disciple

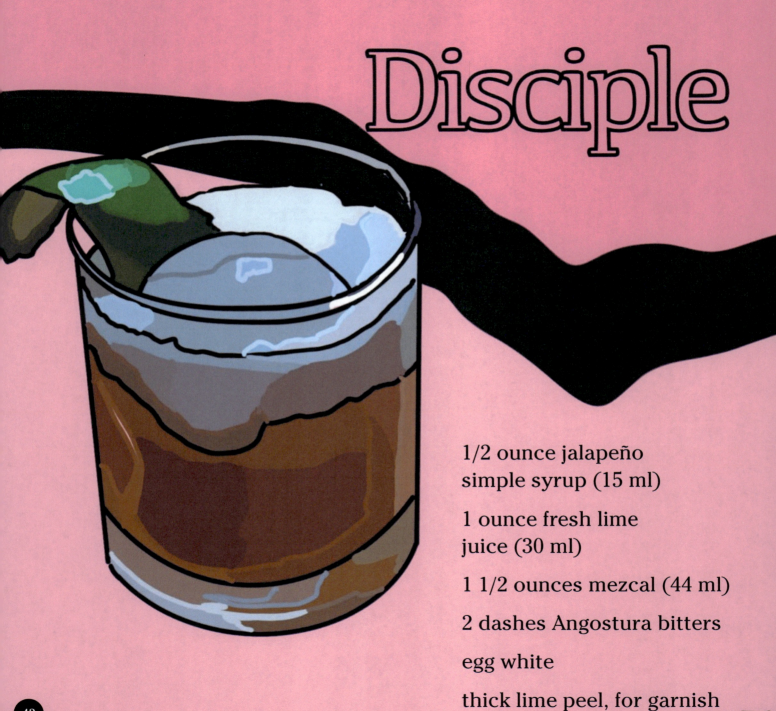

1/2 ounce jalapeño simple syrup (15 ml)

1 ounce fresh lime juice (30 ml)

1 1/2 ounces mezcal (44 ml)

2 dashes Angostura bitters

egg white

thick lime peel, for garnish

I. In a shaker, combine simple syrup, lime juice, mezcal, bitters, and egg white. Dry shake. (Shake without ice.)
II. *Now* add ice, shake vigorously and strain into a rocks glass over ice.
III. Express lime zest over cocktail. (Twist lime peel to "express" citrus over cocktail [outer peel facing drink].)
IV. Garnish with lime peel.

Here's another good one for that jalapeño simple syrup. It does add a little spiciness, but the sugar balances it out perfectly and, in my opinion, totally makes the drink. I absolutely recommend premaking simple syrups and just bottling them up and putting them in your fridge; it'll save you steps down the road. If you want to be able to get away without making jalapeño simple syrup, just substitute it for regular simple syrup and add a few slices of jalapeño before shaking.

Did You Know?

Jalapeño is another one of our ingredients that comes packed with health benefits! The capsaicin in the jalapeño actually comes with anti-bacterial, anti-diabetic, and anti-carcinogenic properties, just to name a few!

Aloe Boa

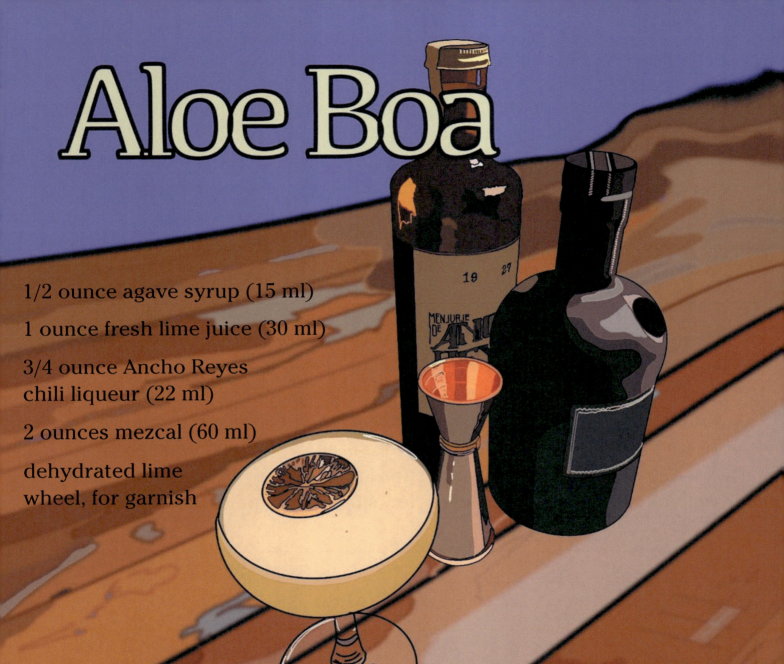

1/2 ounce agave syrup (15 ml)

1 ounce fresh lime juice (30 ml)

3/4 ounce Ancho Reyes chili liqueur (22 ml)

2 ounces mezcal (60 ml)

dehydrated lime wheel, for garnish

I. In a shaker, combine agave syrup, lime juice, chili liqueur, and mezcal.
II. Shake and strain into a chilled coupe (or martini glass).
III. Garnish with dehydrated lime wheel.

It might sound like a cocktail you'd find at a summer birthday party at your mom's friend's house, but this original mezcal libation might just surprise you. And no, there's no aloe vera involved. Misleading right? This is a drink that began with aloe vera simple syrup, which became aloe vera liqueur, before chili liqueur became part of the mix. But the name stuck. (Ancho Reyes Verde is also a great option!)

Did you know?

Ancho Reyes chili liqueur is based off of an early recipe from Puebla, Mexico, dating back to the year 1927. Puebla is known for its ancho chiles, a type of dried and smoked poblano pepper.

White Russian

1/2 ounce Kahlua (15 ml)

1 1/2 ounces vodka (44 ml)

milk

I. In a rocks glass, combine Kahlua and vodka.
II. Add ice. Top off with milk. No garnish.

The Big Lebowski. Enough said, right? I watched that movie a hundred times back in the day, and when I turned twenty-one, that was my drink. The term *Russian* mainly refers to vodka being the main ingredient. Some use cream or even whipped cream; I like mine with milk, but that's just like my opinion, man. The White Russian was conceived in 1949 by Belgian bartender Gustave Tops, right alongside the Black Russian at the Hotel Metropole in Brussels.

Did You Know?

You can also make this cocktail a little different than your normal expected White Russian by making it a Dirty Russian with chocolate milk. Or your classic Black Russian, same as the white but without milk or cream. Put on *The Big Lebowski* and pour yourself a White Russian, man.

Moscow Mule

1/2 ounce fresh
lime juice (15 ml)

2 ounces vodka
(60 ml)

3 dashes
Angostura bitters

ginger beer

lime wheel,
for garnish

I. In a shaker, combine lime juice, vodka, and bitters.
II. Shake and strain into a copper mug over ice.
III. Top with ginger beer.
IV. Garnish with lime wheel.

Another personal favorite vodka cocktail is the Moscow mule. It's only got a few ingredients, but that might be what has helped it stay relevant behind the bar for so many years. The 1940s are when this cocktail got its start: 1941 to be exact. Let's start with Sophie Berezinski creating two thousand copper mugs that she didn't need. She said, "Okay, never mind, I'm going to the US," taking along that new collection of copper mugs. She teamed up with her new partners—a vodka distributor and a ginger beer salesman—and the rest was history.

Did You Know?

Drinking out of a copper cup has actually been known to have certain health benefits. Although unproven, it is said to improve brain function, slow aging, and reduce inflammation, among other things. Studies also show that drinking water out of a copper cup kills bacteria.

Bloody Mary

kosher salt
1/2 ounce fresh lime juice
(15 ml)
1/2 ounce Worcestershire
sauce (15 ml)
small bar spoon horseradish
3 dashes Tabasco
1 1/2 ounces vodka (44 ml)
Bloody Mary mix
Clamato
long celery stick
lime wedge, for garnish
lemon wedge, for garnish
onion, for garnish
olive, for garnish
bacon strip, for
garnish

I. Salt rim of a pint glass.
II. Add lime juice, Worcestershire, horseradish, Tabasco, and vodka.
III. Add a long celery stick as garnish. *Then*, fill glass with ice.
IV. Add Bloody Mary mix (leave room on top!).
V. Top off with Clamato. (Mix with celery stick.)
VI. Garnish with lime and lemon wedges, onion, and olive on a bamboo pick. Stab pick through a bacon strip and into celery to hold together as a garnish.

Part of the fun of a Bloody Mary is being able to fancy it up and make it your own. We can keep this a quarantine-friendly version and just go for the bloody premix and dump vodka in a glass, but I say let's get down on this one. History says Fernand Petiot claimed to have invented the Bloody Mary in 1921 at the New York Bar in Paris. Whether you're at brunch with your friends or stuck at home during lockdown, a Bloody Mary is always a great way to kick off the weekend. Millions of fans can't be wrong!

Did You Know?

The Bloody Mary is known as a great hangover cure. Yes, there are multiple hangover cures in this book, but the Bloody Mary might just be *the* cure. Bloody Marys come with a vegetable base to calm the stomach, plenty of salt to replace lost electrolytes, and alcohol to cure your aching head, which is why it needs to be *your* next choice for the morning after.

Dirty Vodka Martini

1/2 ounce olive juice (15 ml)

1/4 ounce dry vermouth (7 ml)

2 1/2 ounces vodka (75 ml)

olive, for garnish

I. In a mixing glass, combine olive juice, vermouth, and vodka.
II. Add ice, stir for 20 seconds and strain into a chilled martini glass.
III. Garnish with olive on a bamboo pick.

I enjoy my vodka martinis dirty—and that's coming from someone who hates olives. Although the history is unclear, many classic cocktails can be traced back to the father of mixology, Jerry Thomas, in the 1800s. That seems to be the most reliable story, although there have been endless claims recorded since its inception. In time, vodka martinis started gaining popularity over gin, stemming from lack of smell and taste. With or without olive juice, this is a solid choice.

Did You Know?

When you shake a martini, it actually creates a weaker drink. Stirring your drink will create a clearer cocktail and a stronger martini. If you like a shaken martini, more power to ya, but it does tend to over dilute the cocktail while also making it cloudier.

Long Island Iced Tea

3/4 ounce simple syrup (22 ml)

1 ounce fresh lemon juice (30 ml)

1/2 ounce Cointreau (or triple sec) (15 ml)

1/2 ounce vodka (15 ml)

1/2 ounce gin (15 ml)

1/2 ounce rum (15 ml)

1/2 ounce tequila (15 ml)

Coke

lemon wheel, for garnish

I. In a shaker, combine simple syrup, lemon juice, Cointreau, vodka, gin, rum, and tequila.
II. Shake and strain into a collins glass over ice.
III. Top off with Coke.
IV. Garnish with lemon wheel.

The Long Island is a cocktail with a history, so to speak, of sneaking up on you. They say after only a couple, that's all she wrote. It's commonly made with gin, vodka, rum, and Cointreau or triple sec, but we're going to throw tequila in there as well. The Long Island was invented in 1972 at a cocktail competition by a bartender who needed an entry for 'an original cocktail with triple sec in it'. As you can imagine, it was an instant success and has been a hugely popular cocktail around the world ever since.

Did You Know?

A Long Island iced tea is another cocktail that has a bunch of cousins. One of my favorite variations is a Texas tea, coming in with an added half ounce of bourbon. Tokyo tea? Add a half ounce of melon liqueur. Or take the Long Island and substitute Coke for cranberry juice to get a Long Beach iced tea. Now get out there and make some iced teas, you badass bartender you.

The Violator

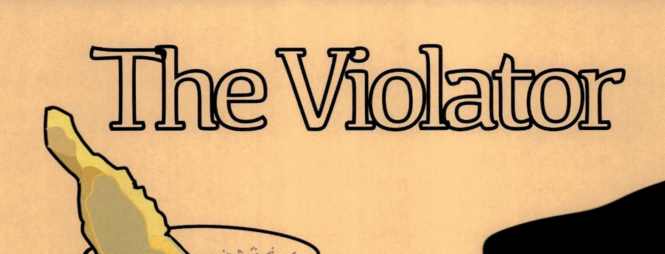

1/2 ounce raspberry syrup (15 ml)

3/4 ounce fresh lemon juice (22 ml)

1/4 ounce Chambord (7 ml)

1 1/2 ounces mandarin vodka (44 ml)

soda water

lemon peel, for garnish

I. In a shaker, combine raspberry syrup, lemon juice, Chambord, and vodka.
II. Shake and strain into a collins glass over ice.
III. Top with soda water.
IV. Express lemon zest over cocktail. (Twist lemon peel to "express" citrus over cocktail [outer peel facing drink].)
V. Garnish with lemon peel.

Originally intended as a summertime drink, this one has stayed close, even throughout quarantine. Fun fact: I was actually on a soccer team when I was seven years old called the Violators. That's correct. I don't know whose dad let us call our team that, but alas, the name lives on. Get violated with this tasty cocktail.

Did you know?

Vodka actually comes from the Slavic word *voda*, which means "water!" The first time that "vodka" was ever mentioned was in Poland way back in 1405!

Spirit Crusher

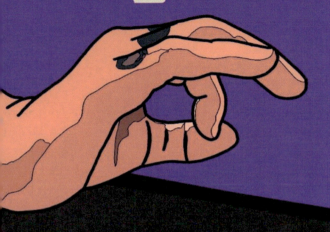

1/2 ounce peach liqueur (15 ml)

2 ounces grapefruit vodka (60 ml)

pineapple juice

1/2 ounce grenadine (15 ml)

3 dashes Fee Brothers
rhubarb bitters

dehydrated blood orange
slices, for garnish

edible flower, for garnish

I. In a mason jar, combine peach liqueur, grapefruit vodka, pineapple juice, ice, and finally grenadine and bitters on top.
II. Garnish with dehydrated blood orange slices and an edible flower.

The Spirit Crusher is always a fun one. And another with room for interpretation. I like mine with grapefruit vodka and peach liqueur, but if you don't have that at your immediate disposal, and you've got some other fruity vodkas lying around, don't be afraid to give one a try! Almost has a mai tai kind of look, but if I've got a choice, I always end up going with the Spirit Crusher. Make sure you have your rhubarb bitters ahead of time, cause that's what makes this drink take flight!

Did you know?

Originally, Spirit Crusher is a song by the band Death, however, this one isn't as threatening as you might think. Actually the opposite. If you're feeling snazzy, you can throw all this into the blender with the addition of a cup of ice and make your frozen cocktail in a martini glass! There are quite a few spirit-forward drinks in here that don't allow extra steps like this, but it suits the Spirit Crusher perfectly.

Negroni

1 ounce sweet vermouth (30 ml)

1 ounce Campari (30 ml)

1 ounce gin (30 ml)

3 rocks

orange peel, for garnish

I. In a rocks glass, combine sweet vermouth, Campari, and gin.
II. Add rocks and stir for 20 seconds.
III. Express orange zest over cocktail. (Twist orange peel to "express" citrus over cocktail [outer peel facing drink].)
IV. Garnish with orange peel.

This is another amazing classic—and with good reason. The negroni has only three ingredients in equal parts—gin, sweet vermouth, and Campari—and they balance each other perfectly. The negroni originated in Florence, Italy, in 1919. Count Camillo Negroni, originally a fan of the Americano cocktail, had the bartender at Café Casoni switch things up by putting gin in place of soda and an orange peel in place of lemon. This is another classic to impress anyone at your bar, bartenders included.

Did You Know?

With only three main ingredients in equal parts, a negroni is one of those cocktails that makes it easy to come up with your own spin-off, which is why we already have a million different variations. Try it with some Antica vermouth; switch up the gin for whiskey to make it a boulevardier; put in a blood orange peel garnish or a flamed orange peel; throw a piece of basil in there and some seasoning on top; substitute Aperol for Campari ... the possibilities are endless.

Gin Martini

1/4 ounce dry vermouth (7 ml)

2 1/2 ounces gin (75 ml)

lemon peel, for garnish

I. In a mixing glass, combine vermouth and gin.
II. Add ice, stir for 20 seconds and strain into a chilled martini glass.
III. Express lemon zest over cocktail. (Twist lemon peel to "express" citrus over cocktail [outer peel facing drink].)
IV. Garnish with lemon peel.

Another great recognizable classic all over the world is the martini: a gin martini, to be exact. The history of the martini is unclear, but it was pretty recognizable by the Roaring Twenties. The 1922 version was made with a 2-to-1 gin-to-vermouth ratio, and the vermouth measurement has gotten less and less ever since. Some even prefer to add zero vermouth for a dry martini. It's the perfect quarantine cocktail, with only a couple of ingredients.

Did You Know?

Everybody seems to view James Bond and *Casino Royale* as the originators of the martini, but the word actually was taken from a German composer named Johann Paul Aegidius Schwartzendorf who changed his name to Johann Paul Égide *Martini* in 1758 after emigrating to France. People from around the world originally learned about his favorite drink from his biography, which allowed the cocktail to take on a life of its own.

Gin Rickey

1/2 ounce fresh
lime juice (15 ml)

1 1/2 ounces
gin (44 ml)

soda water

lime wheel,
for garnish

I. In a collins glass, combine lime juice and gin.
II. Fill with ice, top with soda water.
III. Garnish with lime wheel.

With only gin, lime juice, and soda water, the gin rickey is a super-easy cocktail to make. It's been around for a long time. The story goes that in 1883, the gin rickey came into existence out of the Shoomaker's Bar, where a hungover patron asked the bartender to add a half a lime to a bourbon and soda. Yes, originally it was made with bourbon! It was normal to order it with any type of liquor before gin became the expected spirit. The gin rickey is another quick and easy concoction and it's absolutely delicious.

Did You Know?

F. Scott Fitzgerald, known for such works as *The Curious Case of Benjamin Button* in 1922 and *The Great Gatsby* in 1925, was also known for his love of not only gin, but the gin rickey itself. And it actually shows up in *The Great Gatsby* in chapter 7!

Silver Fizz

3/4 ounce simple syrup (22 ml)

1 ounce fresh lemon juice (30 ml)

2 ounces gin (60 ml)

egg white

soda water

I. In a shaker, combine simple syrup, lemon juice, gin, and egg white. Dry shake. (Shake without ice.)
II. *Now* add ice, shake and strain into an empty collins glass. (No ice in finished cocktail.)
III. Top with soda water. No garnish.

A silver fizz is actually the same as a *gin fizz*, but with the addition of egg white. (A gin fizz is basically a Tom Collins without ice.) The first version of this drink was known simply as a *fiz* and was introduced in 1887 in Jerry Thomas' *The Bartenders Guide.* Thanks again, Jerry. Another classic New Orleans cocktail, the gin fizz eventually became so popular that bars would need to hire more bartenders to take turns shaking them! I've never actually seen the silver fizz on any bar menu, but it truly is a beautiful, clean looking classic cocktail that should be your next choice.

Did You Know?

You can create a fizz in different styles by, for example, adding a whole egg for a royal fizz. Yes, that is a thing! Golden fizz comes with just the egg yolk, and a green fizz comes with no egg white, and a dash of crème de menthe. Another cocktail that has been around for quite some time, so of course, has many different variations. Give each of them a try or create your own version!

Aviation

3/4 ounce fresh
lemon juice (22 ml)

1/2 ounce maraschino
liqueur (15 ml)

1/4 ounce crème
de violette (7 ml)

2 ounces gin (60 ml)

maraschino cherry,
for garnish

I. In a shaker, combine lemon juice, maraschino liqueur, crème de violette, and gin.
II. Shake and strain into a chilled coupe (or martini glass).
III. Garnish with cherry on a bamboo pick.

Ahh, the aviation—a beautiful handcrafted cocktail with gin, lemon juice, maraschino liqueur, and crème de violette. This is a sexy drink and a solid choice, if I do say so myself. If you can get your hands on a bottle of crème de violette, you'll be throwing all kinds of fancy-pants drinks together like nobody's business. Drink first, think later. Just in this case, not in general. The aviation dates back to 1916 and a book titled *Recipes for Mixed Drinks* by Hugo Ensslin, one of the last bar books released before Prohibition.

Did You Know?

Ryan Reynolds is actually partially responsible for bringing the cocktail back since acquiring a stake in Aviation Gin in 2018. Thanks, Ryan!

The Last Word

3/4 ounce fresh
lime juice (22 ml)

3/4 ounce maraschino
liqueur (22 ml)

3/4 ounce green
Chartreuse (22 ml)

3/4 ounce gin (22 ml)

I. In a shaker, combine lime juice, maraschino liqueur, Chartreuse, and gin.
II. Shake and strain into a chilled coupe (or martini glass). No garnish.

The last word is another great classic cocktail. I always felt that it was down the same alley as an aviation, although they taste completely different. We'll leave out the crème de violette on this one. The last word comes with gin and maraschino liqueur, just like the aviation cocktail, but with lime juice in place of lemon. —and this one has green Chartreuse, another weird ingredient. If you can track it down, it'll be an exception to the quarantine rule. Originally developed at the Detroit Athletic Club, the last word is another cocktail straight from Prohibition times. It was featured in *Bottoms Up* by a Ted Saucier in 1951. This classic libation is highly recommended.

Did You Know?

Green Chartreuse is the special ingredient in this bad boy, and it's what makes this one stand out even among other classics. It's story begins in the year 1605. Many people believed it to be an elixir for a good long life. Green Chartreuse comes with 130 plus botanicals, but the recipe and its ingredients are heavily guarded. At some point, monks eventually got a hold of it, and legend has it that only two monks on earth know the recipe. They are not allowed to be in the same city at the same time just in case anything were to happen. Barroom folklore? No way; drink Chartreuse.

Gimlette

rosemary sprig

1/2 ounce simple syrup (15 ml)

1 ounce fresh lime juice (30 ml)

1 1/2 ounces gin (44 ml)

1 dash Fee Brothers peach bitters

lime peel, for garnish

I. In a shaker, combine rosemary sprig, simple syrup, lime juice, gin, and bitters.
II. Shake and double-strain into a chilled coupe (or martini glass).
III. Express lime zest over cocktail. (Twist lime peel to "express" citrus over cocktail [outer peel facing drink].)
IV. Garnish with lime peel.

A spin on the gimlet. I've always been a fan of gimlets. Some like it the old-school way with lime cordial, but enjoy mine with fresh lime juice. The original gimlet cocktail dates back to the year 1928, coming in with equal parts gin and lime cordial. The *gimlette's* flavor profile turns out to be quite different! Ours will be shaken with a rosemary sprig and a dash of peach bitters. Even with five ingredients, it's a super-quick and easy beverage to conquer at home, and a personal favorite.

Did you know?

The word "gimlet" was very first used in 1928 as a tool for drilling small holes! It was also used as a word to describe something as sharp or piercing!

Clover Club Cocktail

1/2 ounce raspberry syrup (15 ml)

1/2 ounce fresh lemon juice (15 ml)

1/2 ounce dry vermouth (15 ml)

1 1/2 ounces gin (44 ml)

1/4 ounce egg white (7 ml)

raspberry, for garnish

I. In a shaker, combine raspberry syrup, lemon juice, dry vermouth, gin, and egg white. Dry shake. (Shake without ice.)
II. *Now* add ice, shake vigorously and double-strain into a chilled coupe (or martini glass).
III. Garnish with raspberry on a bamboo pick.

This one stands out to me as a cocktail among the others in this book because it gives us a chance to use our raspberry syrup (recipe in back of the book), which definitely puts this cocktail up a level. The Clover Club Cocktail, first made at the Bellevue-Stratford hotel in Philadelphia, is a cocktail all the way from 1896, predating Prohibition. Another cocktail to impress your friends. Even to those that are a little wary when it comes to gin or egg white, which is probably most I would say, this one is always a killer choice and is absolutely beautiful.

Did you know?

You can create your own spin-offs of the Clover Club by creating your own fruit syrups! Follow the recipe in the back of the book, while substituting different fruits etc. in place of raspberry! There are some amazing original possibilities!

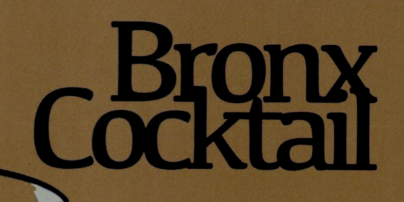

Bronx Cocktail

1 ounce orange juice (30 ml)

1/4 ounce sweet vermouth (7 ml)

1/4 ounce dry vermouth (7 ml)

1 1/2 ounces gin (44ml)

I. In a shaker, combine orange juice, vermouths, and gin.
II. Shake and strain into a chilled coupe (or martini glass). No garnish.

The Bronx cocktail is a great one that got a really early start back in 1905, although the original creator is a bit of a mystery. Some say this one was actually created in Philadelphia and brought back to New York by a Bronx restaurateur. Made popular prior to Prohibition in the United States, this cocktail is basically a perfect gin martini, but with a splash of orange juice, which is what makes this one quite different from a lot of other drinks from around this time period.

Did you know?

You can drop an egg yolk into the shaker to get a Golden Bronx! Or maybe give the Will Rogers cocktail a try! Shake 2 ounces gin with 1 ounce dry vermouth, 1 ounce orange juice, and a bar spoon of Cointreau.

Sidecar

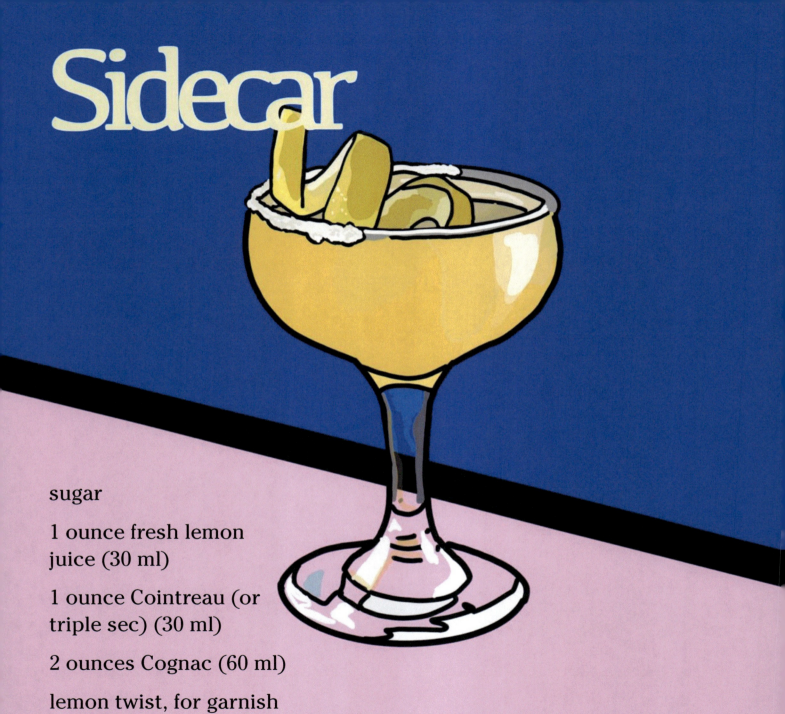

sugar

1 ounce fresh lemon juice (30 ml)

1 ounce Cointreau (or triple sec) (30 ml)

2 ounces Cognac (60 ml)

lemon twist, for garnish

I.   Sugar half the rim of a chilled coupe (or martini glass).
II. In a shaker, combine lemon juice, Cointreau, and Cognac.
III. Shake and strain into glass.
IV. Garnish with lemon twist.

Here's one that I don't get the opportunity to make that often, although it is a terrific cocktail. The sidecar is another classic that's already quarantine-ready with only a few ingredients. The long and short of it is two parts Cognac, one part Cointreau, and one part lemon juice. The Ritz Hotel actually claims that it was the first to pull this one together, although the paper trail gets difficult to follow, as it has been mentioned in numerous publications since the 1920s. Another quick, easy, personal favorite.

Did You Know?

The sidecar is another one of those cocktails that has many different versions, and by just swapping out one ingredient, you can end up with a completely different beverage. Between the sheets? Add rum to the mix! A vodka sidecar? Substitute Cognac for vodka!

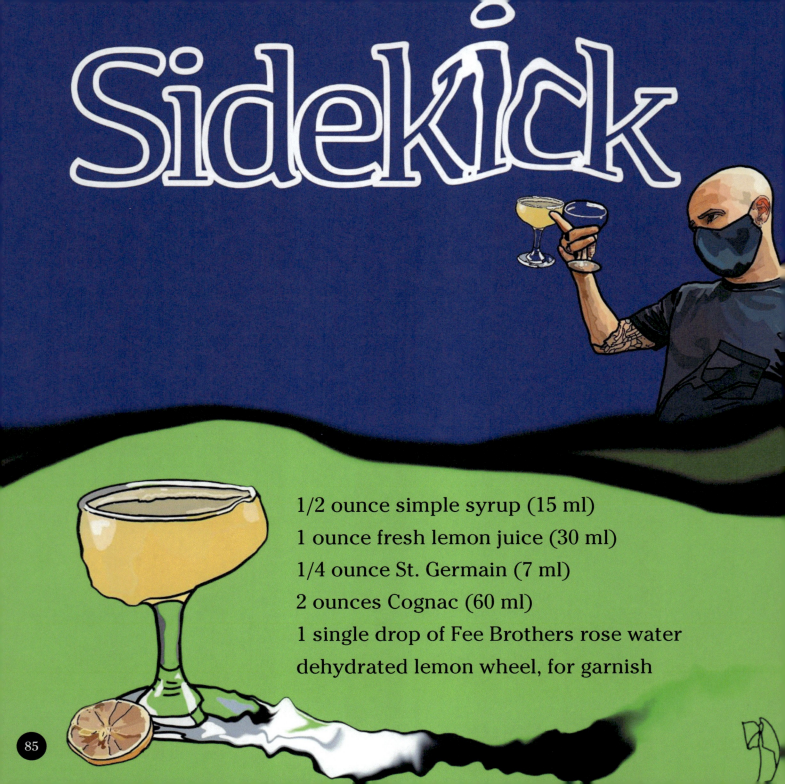

Sidekick

1/2 ounce simple syrup (15 ml)

1 ounce fresh lemon juice (30 ml)

1/4 ounce St. Germain (7 ml)

2 ounces Cognac (60 ml)

1 single drop of Fee Brothers rose water

dehydrated lemon wheel, for garnish

I.   In a shaker, combine simple syrup, lemon juice, St. Germain, Cognac, and rose water.
II. Shake and strain into a chilled coupe (or martini glass).
III. Garnish with dehydrated lemon wheel.

A spin on a sidecar. Substituting St. Germain and a drop of rose water for Cointreau are what help soften this drink out a little bit. A perfect drink to put the rest of that bottle of Cognac to the test.

Did you know?

Cognac is a brandy that is named after the Cognac commune in France. The grapes that are used to make Cognac are grown in the surrounding wine-growing region. It is then twice-distilled in copper pot stills and aged for two years minimum in French oak barrels.

Brandy Alexander

3/4 ounce half and half or cream (22 ml)

3/4 ounce brown crème de cacao (22 ml)

1 1/2 ounces Cognac (44 ml)

ground nutmeg, for garnish

I. In a shaker, combine half and half, crème de cacao, and Cognac.
II. Shake and strain into a chilled coupe (or martini glass).
III. Sprinkle ground nutmeg over cocktail for garnish.

The Brandy Alexander is another cocktail with an unclear start. It has been made for over a hundred years. With stories of the drink popping up at a wedding in England in 1922, to it being named after a Russian tsar, there's a lot to choose from. It's really more of a chocolate martini than anything, but without vodka or gin. Regardless of what class this drink falls under, the Brandy Alexander has earned its place as an OG cocktail and is here to stay.

Did You Know?

Brandy Alexander was actually known as one of John Lennon's favorite cocktails! He called it his milkshake. Doesn't that sound appealing? Go make one.

Kalimotxo

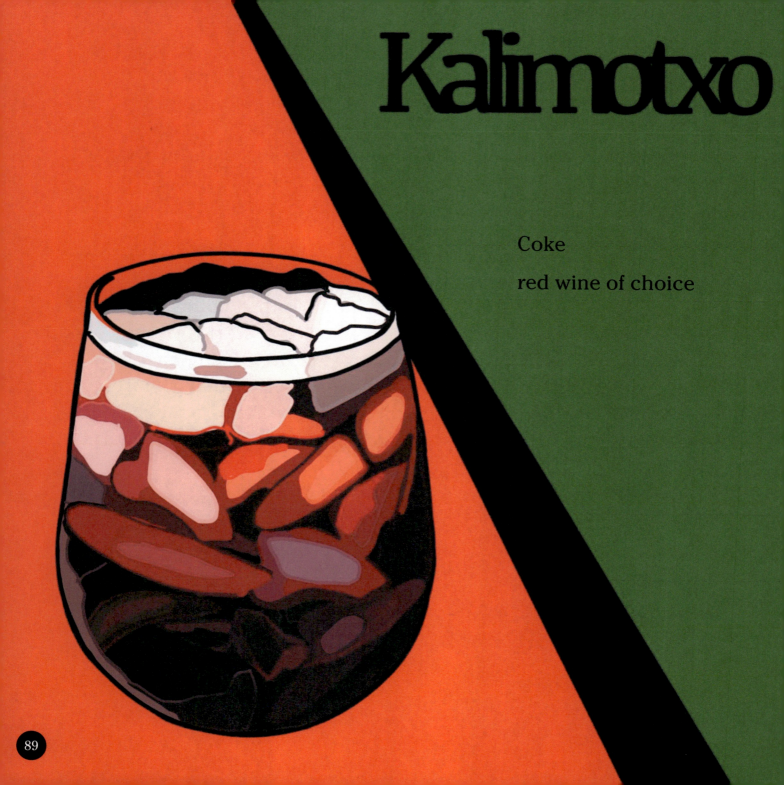

Coke

red wine of choice

I.   Add ice to a wine glass.
II. Add equal parts Coke and red wine. No garnish.

The father of all quarantine drinks, or mother. Just half and half Coke and red wine. The mixture of red wine and Coke was already floating around in the 1920s when Italian immigrants used to mix Coke with their Chianti. However, it wasn't until the 1970s that it became popular in Spain. They brought in two thousand liters of red wine and decided to split it up and mix it with Coke in order to keep the wine from spoiling. And now it's ours: your new quarantine buddy, the kalimotxo cocktail.

Did You Know?

The idea was that saying the ingredients in the drink might be a turnoff, so they needed an attractive name. A friend in the group named Kalimero appeared (who apparently was not a good-looking guy), when another doofus in the crowd decided; "Hey, since *motxo* means 'ugly' in Basque, and Kali is also ugly, let's make that a thing." And so, as fate would have it, poor Kali's name and this drink would be forever intertwined.

Michelada

kosher salt

Tajín seasoning

1/2 ounce fresh
lime juice (15 ml)

1/4 ounce
Worcestershire
sauce (7 ml)

3 dashes Tabasco

Mexican lager

Clamato

lime wedge,
for garnish

I.   Combine salt and Tajín. Dip rim of a pint glass into mixture to coat.
II. Add lime juice, Worcestershire sauce, Tabasco, and 3 ice cubes to glass.
III. Fill with Mexican lager, leaving room on top.
IV. Top off with Clamato.
V.   Garnish with lime wedge.

The famous red beer! I love getting down with a michelada because it is completely open to interpretation. The name comes from the 1960s and a man named Michel Ésper who would ask for it with salt, ice, lime, and a straw. Seems legit. The michelada's unclear history points to another possible start of the cocktail: in Mexico during the Mexican Revolution of 1910. Military leader El General, Don Augusto Michel, would have his soldiers drink Mexican beer with lime and hot sauce thrown in there for character. It really doesn't matter which one is actually true, making a michelada is never the wrong choice.

Did You Know?

National Michelada Day is July 12 every year! Yes, this is an actual holiday! No need to wait for the holiday though, this one is great year round! Today is the perfect day to get reacquainted with this cocktail.

Bellini

1 part chilled white peach puree

2 parts chilled Prosecco

I. In a shaker, combine peach puree and Prosecco.
II. Gently roll ingredients from one shaker tin (or glass) to another a few times to mix ingredients.
III. Pour mixture into a wine flute and top off remaining space with more Prosecco. No garnish.

Most people refer to the Bellini as the perfect cocktail to enjoy on a nice summer day, and you can't really argue with that logic, however, the Bellini is outstanding on any day of the year! Another great quarantine cocktail choice with only two ingredients. This one comes with peach puree, and it's an easy one to make yourself by just blending up a couple peaches (remove the stones) and adding a splash of water to thin out just a bit. The Bellini was introduced to the world in the 1940's out of Harry's Bar in Venice, Italy, by owner Giuseppe Cipriani, and it continues to be a close favorite to many around the world to this day.

Did you know?

The Bellini cocktail was named as a nod to a Giovanni Bellini, 15th century Italian renaissance artist known for his use of colors. The drink's color reminded Cipriani of the toga of a saint in one of Bellini's paintings, hence the name, Bellini.

Disaronno Sour

1/2 ounce simple syrup (15 ml)

1 ounce fresh lemon juice (30 ml)

1/4 ounce Cointreau (or triple sec) (7 ml)

2 ounces Disaronno (60 ml)

2 dashes Angostura bitters

lemon peel, for garnish

I. In a shaker, combine simple syrup, lemon juice, Cointreau, Disaronno, and bitters.
II. Shake and strain into a chilled coupe (or martini glass).
III. Express lemon zest over cocktail. (Twist lemon peel to "express" citrus over cocktail [outer peel facing drink].)
IV. Garnish with lemon peel.

I do remember having a Disaronno sour for the first time and was pleasantly surprised. Another cocktail I can't seem to get enough of! The origins of this classic are cloudy as well, but Disaronno history itself is what makes this cocktail a fun one. Made in Saronno, Italy, Disaronno has been around since 1525, and the company claims that its classic recipe has stayed unchanged the entire time. Disaronno is an amaretto-tasting liqueur, but technically, Disaronno is not an amaretto. Amaretto is made with almonds and Disaronno actually mimics its flavor with various herbs and fruits, but actually contains no nuts of any kind. Add that to the rest of our mix, and you've got quite the cocktail. Another highly recommended concoction.

Did You Know?

Amaro means "bitter" in Italian and *amaretto* means "little bitter!"

Dark 'n Stormy

2 ounces black rum (60 ml)

ginger beer

2 lime wedges (1 as garnish)

I. Start with black rum in a collins glass. Fill with ice.
II. Fill with ginger beer.
III. Squeeze one lime wedge over the cocktail and then throw it into the drink.
IV. Garnish with fresh lime wedge.

Love the story behind this one. Another early start to this cocktail, they say that this one has its roots in Bermuda, and got started just after World War I! The story goes that a sailor came up with the name for this one because the color of the cocktail reminded him of the dark clouds that only a fool or a dead man would sail under. This makes me want one right now. You always hear about the dark 'n stormy, and here it is! A true classic cocktail and a favorite to rum drinkers all around the globe.

Did you know?

This cocktail is popular within the sailing community, and for obvious reasons. The dark 'n stormy, right along with the rum swizzle, are actually known today as the two unofficial national drinks of Bermuda!

Mai Tai

Quarantine Mai Tai

1 ounce white rum (30 ml)
pineapple juice
1/2 ounce grenadine (15 ml)
1 ounce dark rum (30 ml)
pineapple slice, for garnish
2 cherries, for garnish

I. Start with white rum in a pint glass. Fill with ice.
II. Fill the glass three-quarters full with pineapple juice.
III. Add grenadine and dark rum.
IV. Garnish with pineapple slice and cherries.

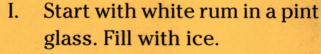

Classic Mai Tai

1/2 ounce fresh lime juice (15 ml)

3/4 ounce orange juice (22 ml)

1/4 ounce orgeat syrup (7 ml)

1/2 ounce Cointreau (or triple sec) (15 ml)

1 1/2 ounces white rum (44 ml)

1 ounce dark rum (30 ml)

pineapple slice, for garnish

cherry, for garnish

I.   In a shaker, combine lime juice, orange juice, orgeat, Cointreau, and white rum.
II.   Shake and strain into a mason jar over ice.
III. Top off with dark rum.
IV.   Garnish with pineapple slice and cherry.

So for the mai tai, I'm going to give the dive bar version first—which also happens to be the same as the quarantine version—made with light rum, dark rum, grenadine, and pineapple juice. I personally prefer our second option, the classic mai tai, which is more what you would have found way back when, but with a couple of modifications. It was created by the owner of Trader Vic's, a tiki restaurant in Oakland, California, in 1944, although there are other stories claiming the mai tai sprung up as early as the 1930s.

Did You Know?

Trader Vic's Bartender's Guide says that the original recipe comes with rock candy syrup! Actually the whole recipe is super interesting and quite different from all of the other recipes in this book. Give it a try! 1 lime, 1/2 ounce orange curacao, 1/4 ounce orgeat syrup, 1/4 ounce rock candy syrup, and 2 ounces Trader Vic's Mai Tai Rum (or 1 ounce dark Jamaican rum and 1 ounce Martinique rum). The taste of a mai tai has changed over the years, but it would behoove you to hunt down some of these ingredients. Your tiki beverage will be that much better!

Mojito

5 mint leaves

1 lime, quartered

3/4 ounces simple
syrup (22 ml)

2 ounces white
rum (60 ml)

soda water

lime wheel,
for garnish

mint sprig,
for garnish

I. In a shaker, muddle mint leaves, lime, and simple syrup. (Use a muddler or the end of a wooden spoon to press the herbs and citrus to extract their oils.)
II. Add rum and ice.
III. Shake and strain into a pint glass over ice. Top with soda water.
IV. Garnish with lime wheel and mint sprig.

Another staple behind the bar. I've actually gotten in the habit of shaking and straining into a pint glass after muddling to keep the mint and lime from getting stuck up the straw and give you a nice easy sipper. Most agree that the mojito got its start in Havana, Cuba; however, South American Indians have used the ingredients in this cocktail as a remedy for illness long before that. Originally, the drink was used for medicinal purposes, to help treat dysentery and scurvy. Who knew so many cocktails had such medicinal purposes! What a time it was to be alive. An amazing refreshment as well as another great day drink.

Did You Know?

Oftentimes, original classic cocktails get the reputation of being an elixir for good health, however, science has actually pointed to the *limes* as being the ever useful ingredient! From vitamin C to antioxidants and other nutrients, drinking lime juice can help to boost your immunity and reduce heart disease!

Uncle Daq

1/2 ounce Demerara syrup (15 ml)

1 ounce fresh lime juice (30 ml)

1/4 ounce maraschino liqueur (7 ml)

2 ounces white rum (60 ml)

2 dashes R&D cherry apple bitters

lime wheel, for garnish

I. In a shaker, combine syrup, lime juice, maraschino liqueur, rum, and bitters.
II. Shake and strain into a chilled coupe (or martini glass). (If frozen, add contents to blender with a cup of ice. Add a few more cubes if not thick enough.)
III. Garnish with lime wheel.

A spin on a daiquiri. Switch it up a little bit by putting some Luxardo (or another maraschino liqueur) in there along with a couple dashes of cherry apple bitters and it'll help spruce up this favorite in a big way! This little concoction is a great choice any time of year, in my opinion. The first daiquiri comes from Cuba in the early 1900's, originally created during the Spanish-American War by an American mining engineer! The daiquiri got its start due to the abundance of limes and rum in the area. Later brought back to the states, the daiquiri didn't gain popularity until the 1940s but has been a go-to for people around the world ever since. You can make a classic daiquiri with just lime, simple syrup, and rum, but even with a couple extra ingredients, this one is perfect for your quarantine bar setup. Uncle Daq will treat you well.

Did You Know?

Ernest Hemingway was purportedly a big rum guy, and the daiquiri was one of his favorites! He explains the look of the daiquiri being similar to that of the sea. —nice and frothy on top and smooth clear waters underneath. "This frozen daiquiri, so well beaten as it is, looks like the sea where the wave falls away from the bow of a ship when she is doing thirty knots."-Ernest Hemingway, *Islands in the Stream*. Well said, Ernest.

Dehydrated Fruits

Most people probably do not own a dehydrator, myself included, so worry not! Put your sliced lemons, apples, limes, apricots, etc. on a piece of wax paper in the oven. Turn your oven down to the lowest possible setting, which is probably around 150 to 175 degrees (mine's 170), for around 8 hours. (Just remember to keep your eye on them, flipping them every two hours.) Pull the fruit out when the pieces look nice and crispy.

Simple Syrups

Step up your cocktails in a big way by making your own simple syrups. Honestly, it's so easy, there's really no excuse not to do it. Just make sure you store them in the fridge, because they will go bad if left out.

A good general way to make a simple syrup is to boil water, add sugar and other ingredients, and simmer for just a couple minutes until the mixture thickens up just slightly before pulling off. It will continue to thicken up after being removed from the heat, so don't leave it on for too long. Here are some other recipes to have fun with. Same basic steps for each.

Simple Syrup

1 cup water (250 ml)
1 cup sugar (250 ml)

I.   Bring water to a boil.
II. Add sugar and stir. Keep at a low boil until sugar has dissolved.
III. Store once simple syrup has cooled.

Demerara Syrup

1 cup water (250 ml)
1 cup Demerara (or brown sugar) (250 ml)

I.   Bring water to a boil.
II. Add sugar and stir. Keep at a low boil until sugar has dissolved.
III. Store once simple syrup has cooled.

Honey Simple Syrup

1 cup hot water (250 ml)
1 cup honey (250 ml)

I.   Combine and stir until sugar has dissolved.
II. Store once simple syrup has cooled.

Ginger Simple Syrup

1 cup water (250 ml)
1 cup sugar (250 ml)
3/4 cup finely sliced ginger (175 ml)

I.   Bring water to a boil.
II. Add sugar and ginger. Keep at a low boil until sugar has dissolved.
III. Remove from heat and let steep for 30 minutes.
IV. Remove ginger, store once simple syrup has cooled.

Jalapeño Simple Syrup

1 cup water (250 ml)
1 cup sugar (250 ml)
2 large jalapeños (sliced)

I.   Bring water to a boil.
II. Add sugar and jalapeño slices. Keep at a low boil until sugar has dissolved.
III. Remove jalapeños, store once simple syrup has cooled.

Agave Syrup

1 cup hot water (250 ml)
1 cup agave nectar (250 ml)

I. Combine and stir until sugar has dissolved.
II. Store once simple syrup has cooled.

Raspberry Syrup:

1/2 cup raspberries (125 ml)
1/2 cup water (125 ml)
1 cups sugar (250 ml)

I. Muddle the raspberries into the sugar and mix thoroughly. Let sit for 30 minutes.

II. Add water and stir until all of the sugar has dissolved.

III. Run syrup through a fine strainer. (Do not boil this syrup on the stove. The raspberries will cook and will change flavor.)

"Sleep late, have fun, get wild, drink whiskey, and drive fast on empty streets with nothing in mind but falling in love and not getting arrested."

-Hunter S. Thompson

In association with…
Aloe Boa
www.aloe-boa.com

MadChair
www.madchairguitarlessons.com

Kettle Black Portraits
www.kettleblackportraits.com

www.oldfashionedmagick.com

Printed in the United States
by Baker & Taylor Publisher Services